Rivers, Lakes, and Ponds

By Eric Braun and Sandra Donovan

STECK-VAUGHN
ELEMENTARY · SECONDARY · ADULT · LIBRARY

A Harcourt Company

www.steck-vaughn.com

Printed and bound in the United States of America
1 2 3 4 5 6 7 8 9 10 WZ 05 04 03 02 01

Photo Acknowledgments
Corbis, 12, 16, 18, 26
Digital Stock, title page, 4, 8, 15, 20, 22, 25
Visuals Unlimited/D. Cavagnaro, cover; Ted Whittenkraus, 28

Content Consultants
Maria Kent Rowell
Science Consultant
Sebastopol, California

David Larwa
National Science Education Consultant
Educational Training Services
Brighton, Michigan

This book supports the National Science Standards.

CONTENTS

Some fish depend on plants in rivers, lakes, and ponds to live.

The Rivers, Lakes, and Ponds Biome

S cientists study parts of Earth to learn more about the whole Earth. Some scientists study parts of Earth called biomes. Biomes are large regions, or areas, that have communities of plants and animals. A community is a group of plants and animals that live in the same place. Rivers, lakes, and ponds make up one kind of biome.

Biomes have different climates. Climate is the usual weather in a place. Climate includes the amount of rain that falls, usual wind speeds, and temperature. Temperature measures how hot or cold a place is. Climate is important because it helps determine what kinds of plants grow in a biome.

Soil, Plants, and Animals

Soil is also important in a biome. Different biomes have different kinds of soils. Many kinds of plants grow in biomes with rich soil. Fewer plants grow in biomes with dry or poor soil. Few plants can live where water and wind carry soil away.

Plants and animals are adapted to their biomes. To be adapted means that a living thing has features that help it fit where it lives. Plants and animals that live in rivers, lakes, and ponds are adapted to water.

Rivers, Lakes, and Ponds

Rivers, lakes, and ponds are found all over the world. In fact, from outer space the world looks like a spider web. The lines of the web are rivers running all over the world.

Three-fourths of the area of Earth is water. Only 3% of this water is in rivers, lakes, and ponds. The rest is ocean. Oceans are huge bodies of saltwater. Most rivers, lakes, and ponds are freshwater. Freshwater does not have nearly as much salt as the ocean does.

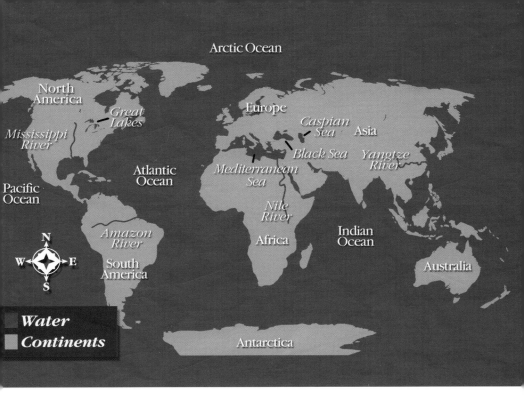

> **This map shows the locations of the major waterways of the world including several important lakes and rivers.**

Ponds and lakes are bodies of still water. This means the water does not move. Rivers are moving water. Many rivers flow into lakes. Eventually, nearly all rivers flow into the ocean.

Large flocks of geese live near lakes and ponds. They eat the fish from the water.

About Rivers, Lakes, and Ponds

Many regions of Earth have rivers, lakes, and ponds. They can be on flat land or in mountains. They can be near dry areas, such as deserts. They can be in very wet areas, such as rain forests. A rain forest is a warm place where many trees and plants grow close together and a lot of rain falls.

Many rivers are found in mountains. These rivers have very cold water that moves fast in the spring. This is from the snow that melts on the mountains. Rivers in warmer regions move more slowly than mountain rivers. Many rivers in warm climates have more plants and animals living in them than cold rivers do.

Rivers

Rivers are bodies of water that move in one direction. There are rivers all over the world. The longest river is the Nile River in Africa. It is 4,132 miles (6,650 km) long.

The beginning of a river is made up of the headwaters. The headwaters can come from melting mountain snow, from a lake, or from another body of water. The headwaters are the coldest and clearest part of a river.

At its middle part, a river usually gets wider. The river water also gets warmer. This is because the sun can warm the water as it spreads out. More kinds of plants and animals live in the middle part of a river.

The end of a river is called the mouth. Usually the river water goes into another body of water, such as a lake or ocean.

At the mouth of a river, the water becomes cloudy from **sediment**. Sediment is rocks, sand, or dirt from the river bottom that mixes with the river water. This makes it harder to see the bottom of a river at its mouth.

This island is in the middle of a river.

Lakes

Lakes are large areas of water. There are both freshwater and saltwater lakes. Oxygen is a gas that animals need in order to live. Freshwater lakes carry more oxygen than saltwater lakes. Because of this, freshwater lakes have more animals and plants than saltwater lakes.

Lakes can be small or large. Very large lakes are sometimes called seas. The world's largest lake is the Caspian Sea. It is 760 miles (1,223 km) wide and is located between Asia and Europe. The world's deepest lake is Lake Baikal in Russia. It is 5,314 feet (1,620 m) deep.

Saltwater lakes are salty, like the ocean. A lake becomes salty because its water **evaporates** faster than it is replaced. Evaporate means to change from a liquid to a gas. The saltiest lake in the world is the Dead Sea. It is ten times saltier than the ocean. It is so salty, no animals can live in it.

One of the reasons lakes are important is that they hold water when there is a lot of rain. This water can be used by people, plants, and animals when there is less rain.

 These are salt formations in the Dead Sea.

The surface of some lakes freezes for part of the year if they are in a cold climate. Most lakes do not freeze all the way through. When a lake is frozen on top, there is still water under the ice. When this water has enough oxygen, fish and other animals can still live there.

Ponds

Ponds are like lakes, except they are smaller. They are also found all over the world. They are mostly freshwater.

Some scientists say the difference between a pond and a lake is that lakes have wind-swept beaches. These beaches are formed when wind blows across the water. Ponds are not big enough for winds to form beaches.

Many ponds have plants living all across them. Plants, such as lily pads, grow well in a pond's shallow water. A lake is too deep for plants to grow, except near the shore.

Some ponds only last for two or three months and then dry up. Large ponds and lakes can last for hundreds of years.

Ponds can be found in cold and hot climates. Some ponds are in very hot places. Animals use these ponds to cool off. Sometimes ponds are found in the tundra. The tundra is the world's coldest biome. It is so cold that the ground freezes. During the tundra's short warm season, some of the frozen ground melts and forms ponds.

These warthogs are drinking water and keeping cool in a pond in Africa.

This picture shows different kinds of weeds that grow in the water.

Plants in Rivers, Lakes, and Ponds

Many different kinds of plants can grow in rivers, lakes, and ponds. Plants release oxygen into the water. They also provide food and shelter for animals.

Most plants that grow in rivers, lakes, and ponds are **rooted plants**. Rooted means that a plant has roots and grows out of the ground. Rooted plants grow mostly along the shore. This is because the water is not as deep there.

Some rooted plants live beneath the surface of the water. These are called underwater weeds. Many underwater weeds have trailing roots that are like a spider web in the water. These trailing roots provide shelter for some fish.

 A cluster of water hyacinths is growing on this pond.

Floating Plants

Other plants do not have any roots. These are called floating plants. Floating plants live on top of the water and do not connect to the ground.

Water hyacinths are floating plants with colorful flowers. Water hyacinths are weeds that have spread to many places around the world. They grow very fast. Scientists know that the plants harm rivers, lakes, and ponds. The water hyacinths keep sunlight and oxygen from getting into the water. This harms fish and other underwater plants. Scientists are working to stop the water hyacinth from spreading.

How Plants Survive

Plants need sunlight to grow in rivers, lakes, and ponds. They use sunlight to make food in a process called photosynthesis. In spring, there are more hours of sunlight each day. This is when most plants start growing.

But many things can make it hard for plants to grow in rivers, lakes, and ponds. Trees or other tall plants can block the sunlight. Also, wind can be dangerous for plants. Wind can make waves on the water's surface. These waves can pull plants from their roots. They can also tear a plant's leaves.

Sometimes rain collects on a plant's leaves and it can sink. Also, leaves can get trapped under the frozen surface of a lake or pond. Only the strongest plants survive in these conditions.

Frogs live both in the water and on the wet shores of rivers, lakes, and ponds.

ANIMALS IN RIVERS, LAKES, AND PONDS

Many different fish, birds, insects, and mammals live in and around rivers, lakes, and ponds. A mammal is a warm-blooded animal with a backbone. Mammals make milk to feed their young. Mammals need to breathe air. Most mammals live on land, but some live in the water.

Some animals, such as fish, live only in the water. Other animals, such as frogs, live both in water and on land. Young frogs that are still growing into adults are called tadpoles. Tadpoles live in the water like fish. Once tadpoles grow into frogs, they live in water or on wet land.

 This bear is catching fish from a river.

Land and Water Animals

Some animals live above the water. Ducks are birds that have webbed feet for swimming in lakes and ponds. The web between their toes helps ducks swim easily.

Other animals live on the ground around the water. Beavers live on river banks. They eat plants and cut down trees to build homes and **dams**. Dams are piles of branches, sticks, and mud that cross a river and slow down the flow of water.

Predators

Predators are the biggest threat to most animals in rivers, lakes, and ponds. Predators are animals that hunt other animals and eat them. The animals that predators eat are called prey.

Snakes are predators that live in and near rivers, lakes, and ponds. Snakes eat frogs and insects. They also eat small mammals, such as mice, that live near water. Some snakes can move quickly and quietly through the water. This is how they sneak up on frogs and other food.

Eagles, osprey, herons, and hawks are also predators to many animals in rivers, lakes, and ponds. These birds of prey eat a lot of fish, frogs, and insects.

Larger animals, such as bears and alligators, also try to catch fish to eat. They wait near the water until fish swim by. Then, they use their claws or teeth to grab the fish.

Adaptation

Animals change over time to make it easier to live in their environments. This changing is called adapting.

Many kinds of birds have adapted to life in rivers, lakes, and ponds. Ducks, swans, and geese have wide, round bodies that make it easy for them to float on water. They also have webbed feet for swimming. They have long necks that bend easily to look for food in the water.

Some birds, such as pelicans, have special mouths called bills made for catching fish. Their large bills expand so that they can scoop water and fish from rivers, lakes, and ponds.

Fish have also adapted to life in rivers, lakes, and ponds. Many fish have dark colored tops and light-colored bottoms. When you look at them from above, their dark body blends in with the bottom of the river or lake. When you look at them from below, their light body blends in with the light from the sky. This helps them hide from predators. Colors, shapes, and patterns that make something blend in with its background are called camouflage.

This pelican is flying near the surface of the water looking for fish to catch.

Some mammals have also adapted to rivers, lakes, and ponds. The platypus of Australia has webbed feet and a bill like a duck. This helps it swim and feel for food at the bottom of a river or pond. Other mammals, such as mink, have special fur that helps keep water off their bodies. This helps them to stay warm in the cold water.

Some people live along the river or on the river in houseboats.

PEOPLE AND RIVERS, LAKES, AND PONDS

People have always lived near rivers, lakes, and ponds. These bodies of water have been important to people for many reasons. One reason is that people need freshwater to live. Also, many people eat fish and other animals that live in and near rivers, lakes, and ponds. People also use the water from rivers and lakes to grow crops on farms.

People also use rivers and lakes to transport things. Transport means to move something or someone from one place to another. Boats travel up and down rivers all over the world and bring people things they need.

These people are picking up trash from along the shores of a river.

Today and Tomorrow

People have done many things to harm rivers, lakes, and ponds. Many rivers and lakes are too **polluted** to swim in or eat from. Polluted means an area has been made dirty, especially with garbage or other things made by people.

Some people pollute by dumping **sewage** in lakes and rivers and ponds. Sewage is liquid and solid waste carried away in sewers and drains. Waste can be what the body does not use or need of food that has been eaten. It can also be garbage, or something left over and not needed.

Rivers, lakes, and ponds also get polluted from **pesticides** and **fertilizers** from farms. Pesticides are chemicals made by people used to kill pests, such as insects. Fertilizers are materials used to help crops grow. Rain washes both pesticides and fertilizers into rivers and lakes.

When water is polluted, people cannot drink or swim in it. They also cannot eat foods, such as fish, from it. Pollution can also cause oxygen to be used up faster than it can be replaced. Without oxygen, everything in the water will die.

People are doing many things to stop pollution. Many countries have laws about what can be dumped into water. Other people are working to save some river, lake, and pond animals. Some of these animals are moved from polluted waters to cleaner waters. People are working together to keep rivers, lakes, and ponds safe for the future.

Glossary

dam (DAM)—a strong wall built across a stream, river, or other body of water to hold back the water

evaporate (i-VAP-uh-rate)—to change from a liquid into a gas

fertilizer (FUR-tuh-lize-ur)—a material put on land to make crops grow better

pesticide (PESS-tuh-side)—chemicals made by people used to kill pests, such as insects

polluted (puh-LOOT-ed)—when an area has been made dirty, especially with garbage or other things made by people

rooted plant (ROOT-id PLANT)—a plant that has roots and grows out of the ground

sediment (SED-uh-muhnt)—rocks, sand, or dirt that has settled at the bottom of a body or water or other liquid

sewage (SOO-ij)—liquid and solid waste carried away in sewers and drains

Internet Sites

Biomes
http://ths.sps.lane.edu/biomes/index1.html

Lakes and Ponds
http://www.twingroves.district96.k12.il.us/
  Wetlands/LakesPonds/LakesPonds.html

Water on the Web
http://wow.nrri.umn.edu

Useful Addresses

National Wetlands Conservation Project
1800 North Kent Street
Suite 800
Arlington, VA 22209

U.S. Fish and Wildlife Service
Publication Unit
1717 H Street NW, Room 148
Washington, DC 20240

INDEX